What Is Government?

by Ann-Marie Kishel

first step nonfiction

↳ Lerner Publications Company · Minneapolis

Do you know what government is?

It is the people in charge
of our country.

Many people work for the government.

They work together to make sure things get done.

Communities have their own governments.

Katherine Harris
Secretary of State
Elections Canvassing Commission

Clay Rol
Director, Division (

State government works for
the people in a state.

Federal government works
for the whole country.

Government helps us.

Our government keeps
people safe.

It makes sure people follow
the laws.

Our government protects us.

It makes sure people are treated fairly.

Our government helps
people.

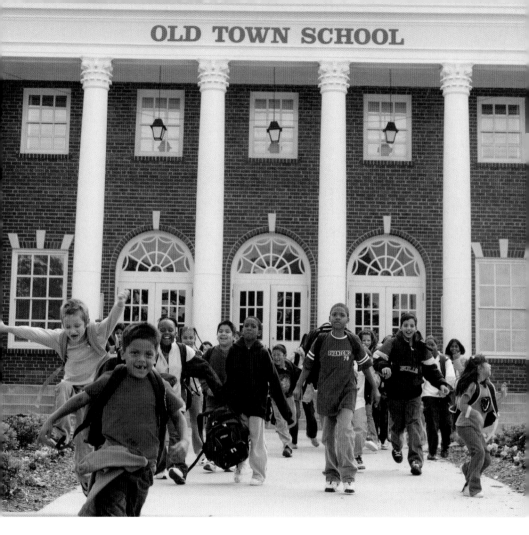

It runs schools and libraries.

We need government.

Government makes our lives better.

The United States

Washington, D.C. ★

Washington, D.C.

Do you know what the capital city of the United States is? It is Washington, D.C. The federal government runs the country from Washington, D.C. The president lives and works in the White House. The Capitol Building is where the U.S. Congress meets. The Supreme Court Building is where the highest U.S. court is held. All of these buildings are located in Washington, D.C.

Branches of Government

 U.S. government has three branches —
legislative (Congress),
executive (president), and
judicial (courts).

 The legislative branch makes laws.

 The members of Congress are called senators and representatives. There are 535 members of Congress.

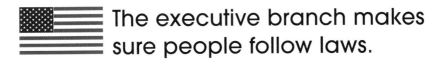 The executive branch makes sure people follow laws.

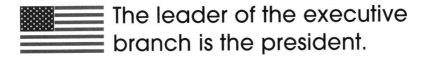 The leader of the executive branch is the president.

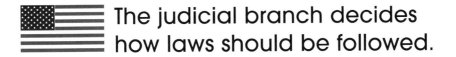 The judicial branch decides how laws should be followed.

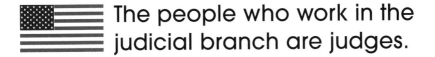 The people who work in the judicial branch are judges.

Glossary

 communities – areas where groups of people live

 state government – the group of people who run a state

 federal government – the group of people who lead and run our country

Index

The photographs in this book are reproduced with the permission of: © Brooks Kraft/CORBIS, front cover, p. 3; © Larry Downing/Reuters/CORBIS, p. 2; © Royalty-Free/CORBIS, pp. 4 (upper left), 9, 13; © Kevin Fleming/CORBIS, pp. 4 (upper right), 12; © Todd Strand/Independent Picture Service, pp. 4 (lower left, lower right), 10, 11; © Mark E. Gibson/CORBIS, p. 5; © Owaki/Kulla/CORBIS, pp. 6, 22 (top); © Reuters/CORBIS, pp. 7, 22 (middle); ©Alex Wong/Getty Images, pp. 8, 22 (bottom); © Chris Hondros/Getty Images, p. 14; © Will and Deni McIntyre/CORBIS, p. 15; © Jeff Dunn/Index Stock Imagery, p. 16; Comstock Images, p. 17. Illustration on p. 18 by Laura Westlund/Independent Picture Service.

Lerner Publications Company,
A division of of Lerner Publishing Group
241 First Avenue North
Minneapolis, MN 55401 U.S.A.

Website address: www.lernerbooks.com

Library of Congress Cataloging-in-Publication Data

Kishel, Ann-Marie.
    What is government? / by Ann-Marie Kishel.
       p.   cm. — (First step nonfiction)
    Includes index.
    ISBN-13: 978–0–8225–6393–8 (lib. bdg. : alk. paper)
    ISBN-10: 0–8225–6393–2 (lib. bdg. : alk. paper)
    1. Political science—Juvenile literature. 2. Political science—United States—Juvenile literature. I. Title.
    JA70.K58 2007
    320—dc22   2006018519

Manufactured in the United States of America
1 2 3 4 5 6 – DP – 12 11 10 09 08 07